Sainsbury's

·RECIPE·LIBRARY·

QUICK & EASY
CHINESE DISHES

Sainsbury's
·RECIPE·LIBRARY·

QUICK & EASY
CHINESE DISHES

Roz Denny

CONTENTS

Published exclusively for J Sainsbury plc
Stamford House Stamford Street
London SE1 9LL
by Woodhead-Faulkner Ltd
Fitzwilliam House 32 Trumpington Street
Cambridge CB2 1QY

First published 1987
Printed and bound in Italy by Arnoldo Mondadori Editore

INTRODUCTION

Chinese cooking is becoming increasingly popular in this country. It isn't only the delicious combination of flavours that attracts us to Chinese recipes. They are also invariably quick and easy to prepare—with an emphasis on fresh and healthy ingredients.

This book is not intended as an authentic guide to the great range of classic Chinese cuisine. It is a collection of Chinese recipes that best suit today's need for quickly prepared or quickly cooked fresh, healthy dishes. The recipes are quite simple and ideal for the novice cook.

COOKING TECHNIQUES

Stir-frying. Small prepared pieces of food are quickly cooked in a little very hot oil for just a few minutes; those foods that need longer cooking are added first. All the foods to be stir-fried should be prepared and ready to add to the wok before you start cooking. It is important to stir the food constantly and toss occasionally. For this reason, woks with one long handle are the easiest to use. A large frying pan can be used if you don't have a wok, but the heat is not distributed so evenly.

Steaming. A traditional Chinese cooking method ideal for today's healthy eating. Good for vegetables, fish, meat and dumplings. Steamers can be stacked on top of each other during cooking; place foods needing longer cooking at the bottom. Woks with a lid and trivet can also be used. Meat and fish are often marinated first. Water or stock can be used for steaming.

Slow Cooking/Braising. Similar to Western braising, after initial stir-frying. Tougher cuts of meat need long or slow braising in rich flavoured stock; fish and vegetables need short braising. The sauces are thickened at the end.

GARNISHES

Many Chinese dishes rely on garnishes to add a finishing decorative touch and colour. The garnishes can be simple, such as coriander sprigs, chopped coriander leaves, lime or lemon slices, or finely shredded spring onion, chilli or carrot, or more elaborate (see below), depending on your experience, patience and time.

Spring Onion Brushes: Trim the green top and remove the white part. Shred the top, leaving 2.5 cm (1 inch) intact. Place in iced water until the shreds open out and curl. **Celery Brushes** can be made in the same way, shredding short lengths of celery sticks.

Carrot Flowers: Trim and scrape the carrot. Using a sharp knife, make about 5 or 6 'V' cuts along the length of the carrot. Cut across into slices.

Cucumber Fans: Cut a slice of cucumber lengthways, about 7.5 cm (3 inches) long, avoiding the seeds. Remove any skin and cut into strips to within 1 cm (½ inch) from the end. Carefully turn alternate strips up to the uncut end. Place in iced water until required. (Illustrated on page 17.)

SPECIAL INGREDIENTS

Many Chinese ingredients are becoming easier to buy, and most of them store for long periods without refrigeration.

Bamboo Shoots: Crunchy cream-coloured shoots of bamboo plant. Available canned or dried; dried shoots need soaking before use.

Bean Curd/Tofu: Blocks of smooth-textured soy bean curd, sold fresh and vacuum packed. Apart from the smoked variety, bean curd has little flavour of its own. The firmer-textured fresh type is more suitable for frying; the vacuum packed is softer and perfect for soups. A very good source of protein and therefore an ideal vegetarian food.

Bean Paste: Fermented, puréed yellow or black beans sold in cans or packs.

Bean Sauce: Yellow or black bean 'ketchup' type sauce for flavouring dishes or to be used as a condiment.

Black Beans: Salted fermented soy beans. Available in cans and packets. Soak packeted beans for 5–10 minutes before use. Check before seasoning, because of their salty nature.

Chestnuts, dried: Soak before use. Fresh chestnuts may be used instead.

Chillies: Especially used in hot Szechwan dishes. Sold fresh, or dried when they are hotter. The seeds are hot too, so discard them if you wish. Chilli juice stings, so take care when preparing; avoid touching your eyes and rinse hands thoroughly afterwards.

Chilli Oil: A red flavouring oil, sometimes containing chilli flakes. Use sparingly, drop by drop.

Chilli Sauce: Hot, sometimes sweet 'ketchup'. Use sparingly.

Chinese Sausage, air-dried: Either pork or pork and liver flavours. Long thin salami-style sausage with slightly sweet flavour. Italian salami could be used with a little sugar added, but the flavour will be different.

Coriander: Also known as Chinese parsley. Has a distinctive flavour. Ordinary parsley can be used as a substitute, but the flavour will not be as good.

Five Spice Powder: A distinctive Chinese flavouring containing star anise, pepper, fennel, cloves and cinnamon. Use sparingly.

Green Vegetables: Numerous leafy greens now available such as pak choi, mustard greens, flowering cabbage as well as Chinese leaf and spinach.

Hoisin Sauce: Barbecue-style sauce. Aromatic and distinctive. Use in dishes or as a condiment.

Mushrooms, dried: Very popular in China. Although expensive per pack, only a few are needed per dish and they store indefinitely. Soak for about 20 minutes in boiling water, discard the stalks and slice the caps for use. The soaking liquor can be used as a stock.

Noodles: An almost bewildering variety which can be interchanged in recipes. Some need quick cooking, others need soaking in boiling water. They can be made from wheat, rice, ground beans or buckwheat. Use thin vermicelli noodles for soups; thicker noodles for main meals or accompaniments.

Oyster Sauce: An alternative to soy sauce, made with oyster juice. Use in meat and fish dishes.

Plum Sauce: A smooth sweet-sour chutney used in meat dishes or as a condiment. Mango chutney without the chunks could be substituted, although the flavour is slightly sharper.

Preserved Vegetables: Several available canned in brine, e.g Szechwan cabbage, mustard greens, red-in-snow. Sometimes spiced. You may wish to rinse before use.

Rice: Two main types: long-grain Patna-type, and shorter-grain sticky or glutinous rice, which holds together in soft mounds for easy eating with chopsticks.

Root Ginger: An indispensable ingredient. It stores well in the cool or can be frozen. Peel sections as needed and grate, chop or shred. Only small amounts are used per dish.

Sesame Oil: Made from sesame seeds. Very aromatic and delicious, adding a distinctive Chinese flavour. Often added to the finished dish. Use moderately.

Shrimps, dried: Used in flavourings for meat, fish, noodle and rice dishes. Soak first in warm water for 15 minutes; use the soaking liquor in the dish.

Soy Sauce, also known as **Shoyu**: Two types are available: light soy sauce is better for light dishes, and dark sauce for those requiring a stronger flavour and colour. It is a fermented mixture of soya beans, wheat or barley, sugar, salt and spices. Naturally brewed sauces are additive- and preservative-free. Where a recipe does not specify light or dark you can use either.

Star Anise: Star-shaped, liquorice-flavoured spice used in braises, red-cooked dishes and marinades. Discard before serving.

Szechwan Peppercorns: Red, aromatic peppercorns used fresh or roasted and ground. Sometimes mixed in equal proportions with salt for a table seasoning.

Tofu: See **Bean Curd**.

Waterchestnuts: Available canned. Have a crunchy texture.

Wonton Skins: Paper-thin squares or rounds of dough, yellow in colour and available ready-rolled, fresh or frozen.

Wood Ears: Rather flavourless fungi used in Chinese dishes to add texture. Soak and use as dried mushrooms.

NOTES

Ingredients are given in both metric and imperial measures. Use either set of quantities but not a mixture of both in any one recipe.

All spoon measurements are level:
1 tablespoon = one 15 ml spoon
1 teaspoon = one 5 ml spoon.

Freshly ground black pepper is intended where pepper is listed.

Fresh herbs are used unless otherwise stated. If unobtainable dried herbs can be substituted in cooked dishes but halve the quantities.

Eggs are standard size 3 unless otherwise stated.

Where chicken stock is specified refer to the recipe on page 8. Vegetarians should use a vegetable stock.

As many Chinese flavourings are quite salty, seasoning should be added at the end of cooking, after tasting.

For information on special ingredients, and alternatives where appropriate, see above and opposite.

Very few dishes are recommended for freezing because the required crisp texture of the vegetables is lost during freezing and reheating.

SOUPS

In China, soups are frequently served between courses to clear the palate. Not only are they very tasty and light, they are relatively quick to put together. But they do need a good homemade stock as the basis—use your own, or make the Chinese Chicken Stock below and freeze in 600ml (1 pint) batches.

CHINESE CHICKEN STOCK

1 uncooked chicken
  carcass, or 8 chicken
  wings
350 g (12 oz) pork spare
  ribs
onion skins or spring
  onion trimmings
carrot skins

2.5 cm (1 inch) cube fresh
  root ginger
150 ml (¼ pint) dry white
  wine
2 tablespoons light soy
  sauce
salt and pepper to taste

Makes 2 litres (3½ pints)
Preparation time: 5–10 minutes
Cooking time: 1 hour
Freezing: Recommended

1. Place all the ingredients in a large pan, add 2.5 litres (4 pints) water, cover and simmer for 1 hour. Strain and cool the stock, then chill.
2. Spoon off the fat from the surface. Use as required.

NOODLE SOUP WITH TOFU

2 tablespoons groundnut
  oil
125 g (4 oz) smoked tofu
  or bean curd, cut into
  1.5 cm (¾ inch) squares
4 spring onions, sliced
1 clove garlic, crushed
75 g (3 oz) mangetouts,
  topped, tailed and
  halved

1.2 litres (2 pints) chicken
  stock
2 tablespoons light soy
  sauce
2 tablespoons dry sherry
50 g (2 oz) instant rice
  noodles
salt and pepper to taste

Serves 4–6
Preparation time: 7 minutes
Cooking time: 7 minutes
Freezing: Not recommended

Illustrated bottom right: Clear Soup with Pâté Wontons and Shredded Greens (page 10)

1. Heat the oil in a wok, add the tofu or bean curd and fry for 2 minutes, turning once. Remove from the wok.
2. Add the spring onions and garlic to the wok and stir-fry for 1 minute.
3. Add the mangetouts, stock, soy sauce, sherry, and salt and pepper and simmer for 2 minutes.
4. Add the noodles and tofu or bean curd and let stand for 2 minutes before serving, reheating gently if necessary.

PRAWN AND CORN SOUP

350 g (12 oz) cooked
    prawns in shells or 175 g
    (6 oz) peeled prawns
    (thawed if frozen)
2 tablespoons groundnut
    oil
4 spring onions, sliced
    thinly
1 teaspoon chopped fresh
    root ginger

1 clove garlic, crushed
900 ml (1 1/2 pints) chicken
    stock
283 g (10 oz) can creamed
    sweetcorn
198 g (7 oz) can sweetcorn
    kernels, drained
2 tablespoons dry sherry
1 teaspoon sesame oil
salt and pepper to taste

Serves 4–6
Preparation time:
5 minutes
Cooking time:
6 minutes
Freezing:
Not recommended

1. If using whole prawns, peel, leaving the tail shells on. Set the prawns aside.
2. Heat the oil in a wok, add the spring onions, ginger and garlic and stir-fry for 2 minutes.
3. Add the stock, creamed sweetcorn, sweetcorn kernels, sherry, sesame oil, and salt and pepper, bring to the boil, then simmer for 2 minutes.
4. Add the prawns, reheat and serve immediately.

CLEAR SOUP WITH PÂTÉ WONTONS AND SHREDDED GREENS

This is where East meets West! I first ate pâté-filled wontons deep-fried, in a Parisian Chinese restaurant. They work equally well simmered in a tasty soup, with shredded greens providing a contrasting crunch.

8 wonton skins
50 g (2 oz) coarse pâté
1.2 litres (2 pints) chicken
    stock
3 spring onions, sliced
    thinly

3 medium-size spring
    green leaves, shredded
1–2 tablespoons light soy
    sauce
2 tablespoons medium dry
    sherry
salt and pepper to taste

Serves 4
Preparation time:
10 minutes
Cooking time:
3 minutes
Freezing:
Not recommended

Illustrated on
page 9

1. Brush the edges of the wonton skins with water. Divide the pâté between them, then fold into triangles, pressing well to seal.
2. Place the stock, spring onions and greens in a large pan, bring to the boil, then simmer for 1 minute. Add the wonton skins and simmer for 2 minutes.
3. Stir in the remaining ingredients. Check the seasoning and serve immediately.

HOT CRAB AND ASPARAGUS SOUP

The 'hot' refers to the chilli sauce—reduce it, if you wish.

6–8 asparagus spears
1.2 litres (2 pints) chicken stock
2 tablespoons oyster sauce
3 spring onions, sliced diagonally
4 button mushrooms, sliced

1 teaspoon chilli sauce
1 teaspoon sugar
few drops sesame oil
125 g (4 oz) fresh or canned white crab meat, drained
salt and pepper to taste

1. Cut off the asparagus tips and set aside. Slice the stalks diagonally.
2. Place all the ingredients, except the asparagus tips and crab, in a large pan and simmer for 5 minutes.
3. Add the asparagus tips and crab and simmer for 2 minutes. Check the seasoning and serve immediately.

Serves 4–6
Preparation time: 5 minutes
Cooking time: 7 minutes
Freezing: Not recommended

EGG FLOWER AND WATERCRESS SOUP

The ultimate nourishing soup. Light, quick and very tasty.
It can even be made in a microwave oven.

*900 ml (1½ pints) chicken
 stock
2 tablespoons light soy
 sauce
1 tablespoon dry sherry
2 tablespoons chopped
 spring onion*

*3 tablespoons roughly
 chopped watercress
 leaves
few drops sesame oil
 (optional)
2 eggs, beaten
salt and pepper to taste*

Serves 4–6
Preparation time:
5 minutes
Cooking time:
5 minutes
Freezing:
Not recommended

1. Place the stock, soy sauce, sherry, spring onion, watercress, sesame oil if using, and salt and pepper in a large
pan and bring to the boil.
2. When on the point of boiling, pour in the eggs, wait a
few seconds, then stir. The eggs should set in ribbons.
Serve immediately, with additional soy sauce if you wish.

PORK BALLS AND PEA SOUP

*FOR THE MEAT BALLS:
175 g (6 oz) minced pork
50 g (2 oz) ham, chopped
1 tablespoon light soy
 sauce
1 spring onion, quartered
1 teaspoon chopped fresh
 root ginger
1 clove garlic, crushed
½ egg white
salt and pepper to taste*

*FOR THE PEA SOUP:
1.2 litres (2 pints) chicken
 stock
2 tablespoons medium dry
 sherry
2 tablespoons light soy
 sauce
75 g (3 oz) frozen peas
TO GARNISH (optional):
parsley or coriander leaves*

Serves 4–6
Preparation time:
10 minutes
Cooking time:
10 minutes
Freezing:
Recommended, at
end of stage 1

1. Place all the ingredients for the meat balls in a food
processor or blender and work together until smooth.
Using wet hands, form into about 18 little balls; set aside.
2. Place the stock, sherry and soy sauce in a large pan and
bring to the boil.
3. Season lightly with salt and pepper, add the meat balls
and simmer for 5 minutes. Add the peas and simmer for
2 minutes.
4. Garnish with parsley or coriander, if you wish, to serve.

FISH DISHES

The Chinese have some delicious fish and shellfish ideas, using inland freshwater fish as well as seawater fish. The beauty of them is that they cook very quickly—many in less than 10 minutes—and need little preparation. I tend to use firm-fleshed fish for these dishes, as they hold together well and the fuller taste goes better with strong flavours, such as soy sauce and ginger.

SALMON TAILS WITH CASHEW NUT AND BACON DRESSING

2 salmon tails, each
   weighing about 500 g
   (1 lb)
1 clove garlic, crushed
3 tablespoons light soy
   sauce
2 tablespoons medium dry
   sherry
2 tablespoons groundnut
   oil
3 spring onions, shredded

1 tablespoon shredded
   fresh root ginger
1 carrot, sliced thinly
2 rashers back bacon,
   derinded and diced
50 g (2 oz) unsalted
   cashew nuts
300 ml (½ pint) stock or
   water (approximately)
1 tablespoon cornflour
2 teaspoons sesame oil
pepper to taste

Serves 4–6
Preparation time:
12 minutes, plus
marinating
Cooking time:
About 10 minutes
Freezing:
Not recommended

1. Slash the salmon tails twice on each side. Place in a polythene bag.
2. Mix the garlic, soy sauce and sherry together. Pour onto the fish, rub well in and leave to marinate for 2 hours.
3. Transfer with a fish slice to a steamer, reserving the marinade, and steam for about 10 minutes; if they don't fit into a steamer together, cook one at a time, cover with foil and keep warm.
4. Meanwhile, heat the groundnut oil in a wok, add the spring onions, ginger, carrot and bacon and stir-fry for 2 minutes. Add the cashews and stir-fry for 1 minute.
5. Make up the marinade to 300 ml (½ pint) with stock or water and blend with the cornflour and sesame oil. Add to the pan and cook, stirring, until thickened. Season with pepper.
6. Arrange the fish tails on a warmed serving plate, spoon over the dressing and serve immediately.

Illustrated bottom
right: Crab Foo
Yung (page 16)

SWEET AND SOUR FISH

1 egg white
1½ tablespoons cornflour
1 tablespoon light soy sauce
1 teaspoon five spice powder
500 g (1 lb) white fish fillets, skinned and cut into cubes
150 ml (¼ pint) groundnut oil
5 spring onions, sliced
1 clove garlic, crushed
1 tablespoon chopped fresh root ginger
3 carrots, cut into strips

¼ cucumber, halved lengthways, seeded and sliced
salt and pepper to taste
FOR THE SAUCE:
4 tablespoons pineapple juice
2 tablespoons medium dry sherry
2 tablespoons wine vinegar
1 tablespoon sugar
1 tablespoon light soy sauce
150 ml (¼ pint) water
1 tablespoon cornflour

Serves 3–4
Preparation time:
12 minutes
Cooking time:
10 minutes
Freezing:
Not recommended

1. Whisk the egg white until frothy, then beat in the cornflour, soy sauce, five spice powder, and salt and pepper. Add the fish and mix well.
2. Mix the sauce ingredients together and set aside.
3. Heat the oil in a wok and fry the fish in 2 batches for 1 minute on each side. Drain on kitchen paper, place on a warmed serving plate and keep warm.
4. Pour off all but 2 tablespoons oil from the wok, add the spring onions, garlic, ginger, carrots and cucumber and stir-fry for 2 minutes.
5. Pour in the sauce and cook, stirring, until thickened. Season lightly with salt and pepper. Spoon the vegetables over the fish with a slotted spoon and serve the remaining sauce separately.

CRAB FOO YUNG

175 g (6 oz) fresh or canned white crab meat, drained
2 tablespoons light soy sauce
1 tablespoon dry sherry
1 teaspoon chilli oil (optional)
2 tablespoons groundnut oil

3 spring onions, sliced diagonally
1 clove garlic, crushed
1 tablespoon chopped fresh root ginger
3 eggs (size 2), beaten
salt and pepper to taste
TO SERVE:
watercress sprigs
sesame oil

1. Squeeze the crab meat to remove any extra liquid. Blend together the soy sauce, sherry and chilli oil, if using, add the crab meat and leave to marinate for 20 minutes.

2. Heat 1 tablespoon of the oil in a wok, add the spring onions, garlic and ginger and stir-fry for 1 minute. Add the crab and heat through. Add the remaining oil.

3. Season the eggs with salt and pepper, pour into the wok and allow to set gently like an omelette, stirring occasionally—do not overstir.

4. Garnish with watercress and sprinkle lightly with sesame oil. Serve immediately.

Serves 2–4
Preparation time: 10 minutes, plus marinating
Cooking time: 4 minutes
Freezing: Not recommended

Illustrated on page 15

SQUID WITH DRIED SHRIMPS AND GREEN PEPPER

500 g (1 lb) squid
2 tablespoons dried
  shrimps
2 tablespoons oyster or
  soy sauce
1 tablespoon dry sherry
1 tablespoon tomato
  ketchup
1 teaspoon cornflour

2 tablespoons groundnut
  oil
6 spring onions, sliced
1 green pepper, cored,
  seeded and diced
1 clove garlic, crushed
salt and pepper to taste
spring onion brushes to
  garnish

Serves 3–4
Preparation time:
15 minutes, plus
soaking time
Cooking time:
7 minutes
Freezing:
Not recommended

1. To prepare the squid, pull off the head and remove the transparent 'quill' and innards. Peel off the skin. Cut the squid body into thin rings. Cut the tentacles from the head just below the eyes. Set aside the rings and tentacles and discard the rest.
2. Soak the shrimps in warm water for 15 minutes. Drain, reserving 2 tablespoons of the water.
3. Mix together the oyster or soy sauce, sherry, ketchup, reserved soaking water and cornflour. Set aside.
4. Heat the oil in a wok, add the spring onions, pepper and garlic and stir-fry for 2 minutes. Add the squid and shrimps and stir-fry for about 3 minutes, until just cooked.
5. Pour in the sauce, mix well and season with salt and pepper. Transfer to a warmed serving dish and serve immediately, garnished with spring onion brushes.

SCALLOPS WITH GINGER SOY SAUCE

This is an excellent first course for Chinese-style or Western meals. Ideally, use fresh scallops with cupped shells. If you can only find frozen scallops, thaw, then steam in small ramekins to collect the delicious juices.

8 scallops
few shreds fresh root
  ginger
salt and pepper to taste
FOR THE SAUCE:
2 teaspoons sesame oil
1 clove garlic, crushed
1 tablespoon grated fresh
  root ginger
2 spring onions, chopped

1 tablespoon light soy
  sauce
1 tablespoon dark soy
  sauce
pinch of sugar
few drops chilli oil
  (optional)
TO GARNISH:
shredded spring onion

1. Blend all the sauce ingredients together and place in a small serving bowl or ramekin.

2. If using fresh scallops, loosen from the shell and trim away any chewy muscle, if necessary. Rinse to remove any grit and return to the shells. Season lightly with salt and pepper and top with a few shreds of ginger.

3. Steam in the shells for about 6 minutes: do this in 2 batches if the scallops are large; if small, steam 2 scallops per shell; if frozen, steam in small ramekins.

4. Remove the shells carefully from the steamer to keep all the juices and arrange on a serving plate with the sauce bowl in the centre. Garnish with spring onion shreds.

5. Each diner should spoon sauce onto the scallops before eating, then drink the juice afterwards.

Serves 4
Preparation time:
10 minutes
Cooking time:
6 minutes
Freezing:
Not recommended

SQUID WITH CORIANDER VEGETABLES

750 g (1½ lb) squid
3 tablespoons groundnut
*   oil*
1 large leek, shredded
1 large carrot, shredded
1 clove garlic, crushed
1 tablespoon chopped fresh
*   root ginger*
125 g (4 oz) button
*   mushrooms, halved*

100 g (3½ oz) bean
*   sprouts*
3 tablespoons light soy
*   sauce*
1 tablespoon medium dry
*   sherry*
2 tablespoons chopped
*   coriander leaves*
salt and pepper to taste
coriander sprigs to garnish

Serves 3–4
Preparation time:
20 minutes
Cooking time:
6 minutes
Freezing:
Not recommended

1. Prepare the squid as for Squid with Dried Shrimps and Green Pepper (page 18). Blanch the rings and tentacles in boiling salted water for 1 minute. Drain and set aside.
2. Heat the oil in a wok, add the leek, carrot, garlic and ginger and stir-fry for 1 minute. Add the mushrooms and bean sprouts and stir-fry for 1 minute.
3. Add the soy sauce, sherry, coriander leaves, and salt and pepper and stir well. Add the squid and stir-fry for about 1 minute until cooked. Transfer to a warmed serving dish, garnish with coriander and serve immediately.

BRAISED MACKEREL WITH PRESERVED VEGETABLES

Chinese preserved vegetables, such as radish or cabbage, can be bought in cans and used either as condiments to be served separately like a chutney, or added to sauces. Some are quite salty, so rinse them first if you wish.

1 large or 2 small
*   mackerel, total weight*
*   750 g (1½ lb)*
2 tablespoons light soy
*   sauce*
2 tablespoons medium dry
*   sherry*
4 dried Chinese
*   mushrooms*
2 tablespoons lemon juice
1 teaspoon caster sugar
2 teaspoons cornflour
3 tablespoons groundnut
*   oil*

2 leeks, sliced thinly,
*   diagonally*
1 clove garlic, crushed
1 tablespoon chopped fresh
*   root ginger*
2 tablespoons preserved or
*   pickled vegetables*
TO SERVE:
½ head Chinese leaf,
*   steamed and tossed in a*
*   little sesame oil*

1. If using one large fish, discard the head and cut the body into 3 or 4 pieces; slash each piece. Slash small fish twice on each side.

2. Mix the soy sauce and sherry together, pour over the fish, cover and leave to marinate for 2 hours. Drain, reserving the marinade, and set aside.

3. Cover the mushrooms with 300 ml (½ pint) boiling water and leave to soak for 20 minutes. Drain, reserving the water, discard the stalks and slice the caps.

4. Blend together the reserved marinade, soaking water, lemon juice, sugar and cornflour. Set aside.

5. Heat the oil in a wok, add the leeks, garlic and ginger and stir-fry for 1 minute. Add the fish and fry briefly on each side to seal.

6. Add the sauce and preserved vegetables and stir well. Cover and simmer for 12–15 minutes, turning once.

7. Serve immediately on a bed of steamed Chinese leaf.

Serves 4
Preparation time:
10 minutes, plus marinating
Cooking time:
12–15 minutes
Freezing:
Not recommended

CHINESE BARBECUE FISH

This can be cooked under a grill or on a barbecue. If cooked on a barbecue, the fish skin becomes beautifully crisp and flavoursome.

4 trout, mackerel or red
*   mullet*
FOR THE MARINADE:
2 cloves garlic, crushed
1 tablespoon chopped fresh
*   root ginger*
2 teaspoons sesame oil
3 tablespoons light soy
*   sauce*

2 tablespoons medium dry
*   sherry*
1 tablespoon lemon juice
1 teaspoon caster sugar
TO SERVE:
shredded lettuce, pak choi
*   or other greens*
1 teaspoon salt
1 teaspoon ground
*   Szechwan peppercorns*

Serves 4
Preparation time:
7 minutes, plus
marinating
Cooking time:
6–8 minutes
Freezing:
Not recommended

1. Slash the fish 3 times on each side and place on a large sheet of foil.
2. Mix the marinade ingredients and pour over the fish, rubbing in well. Cover and leave to marinate for 2 hours.
3. Barbecue or grill the fish, using a medium heat, for 3–4 minutes on each side, brushing with the marinade during cooking.
4. Transfer to a serving dish and garnish with lettuce, pak choi or greens. Mix the salt and peppercorns together and serve separately. Serve hot or cold.

HOT HUNAN PRAWNS

*500 g (1 lb) raw king
   prawns
1 clove garlic, crushed
1 dessertspoon grated fresh
   root ginger
2 teaspoons chilli sauce
1 tablespoon light soy
   sauce
1 tablespoon medium dry
   sherry
1 teaspoon sugar*

*¹/₂ teaspoon cornflour
1 teaspoon sesame oil
2 tablespoons groundnut
   oil
salt and pepper to taste
TO GARNISH:
few coriander leaves
1 small green chilli, seeded
   and sliced into rings
   (optional)*

1. Peel the prawns, leaving the tail shells on. Slit down the
back and discard the dark vein.
2. Mix the garlic, ginger, chilli and soy sauces, sherry,
sugar, and salt and pepper together. Pour over the prawns,
cover and chill overnight or for at least 3 hours.
3. Drain the marinade into a cup and mix with the cornflour and sesame oil.
4. Heat the groundnut oil in a wok, add the prawns and
stir-fry for 1–2 minutes, until just cooked.
5. Pour in the blended marinade, stirring well to heat
through. Serve immediately, garnished with coriander
leaves, and the chilli if you prefer a hotter flavour.

Serves 3–4
Preparation time:
10 minutes, plus
marinating
Cooking time:
3 minutes
Freezing:
Not recommended

FISH BALLS WITH MANGETOUTS

These are quickly made with a food processor or blender.

2 tablespoons groundnut
  oil
175 g (6 oz) mangetouts,
  topped and tailed
2 spring onions, sliced
1 tablespoon chopped fresh
  root ginger
1 teaspoon cornflour
150 ml (¼ pint) chicken or
  fish stock
1 tablespoon light soy
  sauce
salt and pepper to taste

FOR THE FISH BALLS:
250 g (8 oz) haddock fillet,
  skinned
175 g (6 oz) scallops
  (thawed if frozen)
2 spring onions, chopped
1 rasher back bacon,
  derinded and chopped
1 tablespoon medium dry
  sherry
2 tablespoons light soy
  sauce
1 egg white

Serves 4–6
Preparation time:
20 minutes
Cooking time:
About 10 minutes
Freezing:
Not recommended

1. First prepare the fish balls: put all the ingredients in a food processor or blender and work together until smooth. With wet hands shape into 16–18 balls and steam in 2 batches on a lightly greased steamer base for about 5 minutes, until firm. Transfer to a warmed serving dish and keep warm.
2. Meanwhile, heat the oil in a wok, add the mangetouts, spring onions and ginger and stir-fry for 2 minutes.
3. Blend the cornflour, stock and soy sauce together, add to the wok and cook, stirring, until thickened. Season with salt and pepper. Serve the mangetouts and sauce as soon as possible with the fish balls.

QUICK-FRIED FISH IN OYSTER SAUCE

1 egg white
4 teaspoons cornflour
3 tablespoons oyster sauce
500 g (1 lb) firm white fish
  fillets, skinned and cut
  into 4 cm (1¾ inch)
  cubes
150 ml (¼ pint)
  groundnut oil
4 spring onions, sliced
  diagonally
1 clove garlic, crushed

1 tablespoon chopped fresh
  root ginger
175 g (6 oz) short broccoli
  florets
125 g (4 oz) peeled prawns
  (thawed if frozen)
2 tablespoons dry sherry
150 ml (¼ pint) stock or
  water
50 g (2 oz) blanched
  almonds, halved
  (optional)
salt and pepper to taste

1. Beat the egg white, 3 teaspoons of the cornflour, 1 tablespoon of the oyster sauce, and salt and pepper together. Add the fish and mix well.

2. Heat the oil in a wok until very hot. Carefully add the fish cubes one at a time and fry for 2–3 minutes, stirring only occasionally to avoid breaking up the fish. Remove with a fish slice and set aside.

3. Pour off all but about 2 tablespoons oil. Add the spring onions, garlic, ginger and broccoli to the wok and stir-fry for 2 minutes, then add the prawns and stir-fry for 1 minute.

4. Blend remaining oyster sauce, sherry, stock or water and cornflour together and pour into the wok, stirring until thickened. Season with salt and pepper and return the fish, stirring gently. Transfer to a warmed serving dish, sprinkle with the almonds if using, and serve immediately.

Serves 3–4
Preparation time:
12 minutes
Cooking time:
7 minutes
Freezing:
Not recommended

DRUNKEN STEAMED FISH

4 whole fish, e.g. red
snapper, mullet or trout,
each weighing about
250 g (8 oz)
150 ml (1/4 pint) medium
dry sherry
1 tablespoon light soy
sauce
1 teaspoon cornflour
1 tablespoon groundnut
oil

2 spring onions, sliced
diagonally
1 tablespoon chopped fresh
root ginger
250 g (8 oz) broccoli
florets
salt and Szechwan
peppercorns, roasted
and ground, to taste

Serves 4
Preparation time:
10 minutes, plus
marinating
Cooking time:
About 15 minutes
Freezing:
Not recommended

1. Season the fish lightly with salt, fairly liberally with Szechwan pepper. Pour over the sherry, cover and leave to marinate for at least 4 hours, turning once. Drain, reserving the marinade, and set aside.
2. Blend together the soy sauce, reserved marinade and cornflour. Set aside.
3. Heat the oil in a small saucepan, add the spring onions and ginger and stir-fry for 1 minute. Add the blended sauce and bring to the boil. Set aside.
4. Steam the broccoli for 5 minutes, remove and keep warm.
5. Place 2 fish on greaseproof paper in the steamer and steam for about 7 minutes. Arrange on a warmed serving dish. Drain the juices from the paper into the sauce. Repeat with the remaining fish.
6. Reheat the sauce, arrange the broccoli around the fish and pour over the sauce.

HOT CHILLI QUICK-GRILLED FISH

Use trout, mackerel, mullet or whiting for this dish.

2 whole fish, each weighing
350–500 g (12 oz–1 lb)
4 tablespoons light soy
sauce
3 tablespoons medium dry
sherry
4 dried Chinese
mushrooms
1 teaspoon cornflour

1 tablespoon groundnut
oil
1 clove garlic, crushed
8 paper-thin slices fresh
root ginger, 4 cm (1¾
inches) long
4 spring onions, shredded
1–2 large red chillies,
seeded and shredded
salt and pepper to taste

1. Slash the fish twice on each side. Mix half of the soy sauce with the sherry, then rub into the fish. Leave to marinate for 2 hours.

2. Cover the mushrooms with boiling water and leave to soak for 20 minutes. Drain, reserving the water, discard the stalks and thinly slice the caps. Set aside.

3. Cook the fish under a preheated medium grill for about 4 minutes on each side, or until the flesh flakes. Transfer to a warmed serving dish and keep warm.

4. Meanwhile, blend the remaining soy sauce with the cornflour, making up to 150 ml (¼ pint) with the reserved mushroom soaking liquid; set aside.

5. Heat the oil in a wok, add the garlic, ginger, spring onions, chillies and mushroom slices and stir-fry for 1 minute.

6. Pour in the sauce and cook, stirring, until thickened. Remove some of the spring onions and chillies with a slotted spoon and arrange attractively on the fish. Serve immediately with the remaining sauce.

Serves 2–4
Preparation time:
10 minutes, plus marinating/soaking time
Cooking time:
About 8 minutes
Freezing:
Not recommended

MEAT DISHES

Many Chinese meat dishes can be prepared ahead and cooked in under 10 minutes—a situation that would suit those out at work all day. Even those dishes which take longer to cook can be quickly prepared, relying on marinating to impart delicious flavours. The number of servings varies, as you may wish to serve more than one main course dish at a time.

CHAR SHIU

A famous Cantonese 'roast' which can be used on different cuts of pork, although I find it best to choose meat that has a marbelling of fat through it, such as streaky pork rashers or pork shoulder.

500 g (1 lb) streaky pork rashers, derinded, pork shoulder steaks or leg fillet, cut into 7.5 × 4 cm (3 × 1¾ inch) strips
2 tablespoons clear honey
1 dessertspoon sesame oil
FOR THE MARINADE:
4 tablespoons light soy sauce
2 tablespoons medium dry sherry

2 tablespoons hoisin sauce
2 cloves garlic, crushed
2 teaspoons grated fresh root ginger
2 teaspoons clear honey
1 teaspoon salt
pinch of ground cinnamon
TO GARNISH:
coriander sprigs

Serves 4
Preparation time: 10 minutes, plus marinating
Cooking time: 30–35 minutes
Freezing: Recommended, at end of stage 1

1. Mix the marinade ingredients together and pour into a polythene bag. Add the pork, rub well to cover, seal and chill overnight.
2. Remove the pork strips and place on a wire cake rack over a roasting tin of water; the meat should not touch the water.
3. Mix the honey and sesame oil with 3 tablespoons of the marinade and brush over the meat.
4. Cook near the top of a preheated oven, 190°C/375°F/ Gas Mark 5, for 15 minutes.
5. Turn the slices over and baste again. Return to the oven for 15–20 minutes, until glossy and reddish-brown. Garnish with coriander sprigs to serve.

ANTS CLIMBING THE TREES

A wonderful example not only of a very tasty quick Chinese dish, but also of an ingeniously descriptive name! This is an excellent all-in-one meal.

500 g (1 lb) minced pork
2 tablespoons soy sauce
2 tablespoons medium dry sherry
1 clove garlic, crushed
1 tablespoon grated fresh root ginger
1/2–1 teaspoon chilli oil
175 g (6 oz) instant rice noodles
2 teaspoons sesame oil

2 tablespoons groundnut oil
3 spring onions, sliced diagonally
1 air-dried Chinese sausage, chopped
1 teaspoon cornflour, blended with 150 ml (1/4 pint) stock or water
salt and pepper to taste
shredded spring onion to garnish

Serves 3–6
Preparation time: 10 minutes, plus marinating
Cooking time: 7 minutes
Freezing: Not recommended

1. Place the pork, soy sauce, sherry, garlic, ginger, chilli oil, and salt and pepper in a bowl. Mix well, cover and leave to marinate for 20 minutes.
2. Soak the noodles according to packet instructions. Drain, season with salt and pepper and toss in the sesame oil. Place in a warmed serving dish and keep warm.
3. Heat the oil in a wok, add the pork and stir-fry for 3 minutes. Add the spring onions and sausage and stir-fry for 2 minutes. Stir in the blended cornflour, check the seasoning and cook for about 2 minutes.
4. Spoon on top of the noodles and garnish with shredded spring onion to serve.

PORK AND PRAWN WONTONS

These can be steamed or deep-fried and are ideal as appetizers or part of a main meal.

about 36 wonton skins
oil for deep-frying (optional)
FOR THE FILLING:
175 g (6 oz) minced pork
75 g (3 oz) peeled prawns (thawed if frozen), chopped
2 spring onions, chopped

1 clove garlic, crushed
1 teaspoon finely chopped fresh root ginger
2 tablespoons oyster sauce
1 teaspoon sesame oil
2 tablespoons short-sprouted mung beans, or chopped canned waterchestnuts

1. Mix all the filling ingredients together.
2. Brush the edges of each wonton skin with water, put a teaspoon of filling in the centre and either fold over the edges to meet, or draw up into little pouches. Press well to seal.
3. Deep-fry in batches in hot oil for 2 minutes (not suitable for pouches), or steam in batches in a greased steamer for 5 minutes. Drain and serve as soon as possible with the dipping sauces below.

Makes about 36
Preparation time:
15 minutes
Cooking time:
10–20 minutes
Freezing:
Not recommended

Ginger Soy Sauce. Mix 2 tablespoons each light soy sauce and medium dry sherry with 2 teaspoons grated fresh root ginger.
Barbecue Plum Sauce. Mix 2 tablespoons each plum sauce and light soy sauce with 1 tablespoon hoisin sauce.

PORCUPINES

175 g (6 oz) rice
  (preferably sticky or
  glutinous)
3 dried Chinese
  mushrooms
500 g (1 lb) minced pork
50 g (2 oz) canned water-
  chestnuts, chopped finely

3 spring onions, chopped
1 tablespoon grated fresh
  root ginger
1 clove garlic, crushed
2 tablespoons soy sauce
1 egg, beaten
salt and pepper to taste

Serves 4–6
Preparation time:
10 minutes, plus
soaking time
Cooking time:
30–35 minutes per
batch
Freezing:
Not recommended

1. Soak the rice in cold water for 2 hours; drain and shake dry.
2. Soak the mushrooms in boiling water to cover for 20 minutes. Drain, discard the stalks and chop the caps.
3. Mix the pork with the mushrooms, waterchestnuts, spring onions, ginger, garlic, soy sauce, egg, and salt and pepper and shape into 12 balls, with wet hands. With dry hands, roll the balls in the rice, coating well.
4. Place well apart in a steamer and cook for 30–35 minutes, until the rice is tender; this may have to be done in batches. Serve immediately.

OVEN-BAKED SPARE RIBS

1 kg (2 lb) pork spare ribs,
  chopped into 5 cm
  (2 inch) lengths
salt and Szechwan
  peppercorns, roasted
  and ground, to taste
FOR THE SAUCE:
3 tablespoons dark soy
  sauce
2 tablespoons dry sherry

1 tablespoon wine vinegar
2 tablespoons plum sauce
2 tablespoons clear honey
1 clove garlic, crushed
1 tablespoon grated fresh
  root ginger
1 teaspoon five spice
  powder
2 tablespoons finely
  chopped onion

Serves 3–4
Preparation time:
5 minutes, plus
marinating
(optional)
Cooking time:
1½ hours
Freezing:
Recommended, at
end of stage 1

1. Mix all the sauce ingredients together.
2. Place the ribs in a roasting tin, pour over the sauce and mix well. Cover with foil and leave to marinate overnight if possible, for a better flavour.
3. Cook, covered, in a preheated oven, 170°C/325°F/Gas Mark 3, for 1 hour. Increase the temperature to 200°C/400°F/Gas Mark 6.
4. Uncover, stir and return to the oven for 30 minutes, stirring occasionally, until the juices reduce to a syrupy glaze and the ribs brown. Serve hot, with the seasoning.

KIDNEY IN CHILLI PEANUT SAUCE

Lambs' kidneys can be used instead of pigs' kidneys for this dish in which case they need not be soaked and blanched —simply stir-fry for 3 minutes.

*500 g (1 lb) pigs' kidneys,
    skinned, halved, cored
    and membranes
    removed*
*2 tablespoons groundnut
    oil*
*2 leeks, sliced thinly,
    diagonally*
2 cloves garlic, crushed
*125 g (4 oz) button
    mushrooms, quartered*

FOR THE SAUCE:
*3 tablespoons smooth
    peanut butter*
*2 tablespoons light soy
    sauce*
2 tablespoons dry sherry
2 teaspoons sesame oil
4 tablespoons stock
1 teaspoon chilli sauce
1/2 teaspoon sugar
salt and pepper to taste
TO GARNISH (optional):
red chilli slices

Serves 4
Preparation time:
10 minutes, plus
soaking time
Cooking time:
5 minutes
Freezing:
Not recommended

1. Cut the kidneys into bite-size slices, soak in cold water for 15 minutes, then blanch in boiling salted water for 2 minutes. Skim off any scum from the surface, then drain the kidneys thoroughly.
2. Mix all the sauce ingredients together; set aside.
3. Heat the oil in a wok, add the leeks, garlic and mushrooms and stir-fry for 2 minutes. Add the kidneys and stir-fry for 2 minutes.
4. Pour in the sauce, mix well and heat through.
5. Transfer to a warmed serving dish, garnish with red chilli if preferred, and serve immediately.

LAMB WITH COURGETTES AND RED ONION

*350 g (12 oz) lamb neck
    fillet, sliced very thinly*
2 tablespoons dry sherry
1 clove garlic, chopped
*1 tablespoon chopped fresh
    root ginger*
*2 tablespoons light soy
    sauce*
*4 tablespoons water or
    light stock*

1/2 teaspoon sugar
2 teaspoons cornflour
*2–3 tablespoons
    groundnut oil*
1 red onion, sliced
*250 g (8 oz) small
    courgettes, cut into sticks*
salt and pepper to taste
*coriander sprigs to garnish
    (optional)*

1. Place the lamb, sherry, garlic and ginger in a bowl, mix well, cover and leave to marinate for 1 hour.
2. Blend the soy sauce, water or stock, sugar, cornflour, and salt and pepper together; set aside.
3. Heat 2 tablespoons of the oil in a wok, add the lamb and stir-fry for 2–3 minutes. Remove and set aside.
4. Add the extra oil if necessary and stir-fry the onion and courgettes for 2 minutes.
5. Return the lamb to the wok, pour in the sauce and stir until thickened. Transfer to a warmed serving dish and serve immediately, garnished with coriander if wished.

Serves 3–4
Preparation time:
10 minutes, plus marinating
Cooking time:
6 minutes
Freezing:
Not recommended

GINGER BEEF WITH BLACK BEANS

250 g (8 oz) flash-fry steak
1 clove garlic, crushed
1 tablespoon shredded
*   fresh root ginger*
4 tablespoons stock or
*   water*
2 tablespoons medium dry
*   sherry*
1 teaspoon sugar
1 teaspoon cornflour
3 tablespoons groundnut
*   oil*

½ yellow pepper, cored,
*   seeded and sliced*
⅓ cucumber, halved
*   lengthways, seeded and*
*   sliced*
4 spring onions, sliced
*   diagonally*
⅓ × 170 g (6 oz) can
*   black beans*
pepper to taste

Serves 2–4
Preparation time:
6 minutes, plus
marinating
Cooking time:
6 minutes
Freezing:
Not recommended

1. Slice the steak into thin 'fingers'. Mix with the garlic and ginger and leave to marinate for 10 minutes.
2. Blend the stock or water, sherry, sugar, cornflour and pepper together; set aside.
3. Heat the oil in a wok, add the beef and stir-fry for 2 minutes. Remove and set aside.
4. Add the vegetables and stir-fry for 2 minutes.
5. Return the beef to the wok, add the beans and sauce and cook, stirring, until thickened. Transfer to a warmed serving dish and serve immediately.

SLIVERS OF BEEF WITH VEGETABLES

2 tablespoons groundnut oil
500 g (1 lb) rump steak, sliced thinly
1 tablespoon chopped fresh root ginger
1 large clove garlic, crushed
3 carrots, cut into sticks
2 celery sticks, cut into sticks
125 g (4 oz) mangetouts, topped and halved, or baby corn cobs
1 green pepper, cored, seeded and sliced
3 courgettes, cut into sticks
4 spring onions, chopped
125 g (4 oz) button mushrooms
FOR THE SAUCE:
2 tablespoons dark soy sauce
2 tablespoons dry sherry
150 ml (¼ pint) water
1 tablespoon cornflour
salt and pepper to taste
TO SERVE:
50 g (2 oz) unsalted cashew nuts or almonds

1. Blend the sauce ingredients together.
2. Heat the oil in a wok, add the beef, ginger and garlic and stir-fry for 2 minutes.
3. Add the vegetables in the order listed. Stir-fry for a total of 2–3 minutes. Add the sauce to the wok, toss well and cook for 1 minute. Check the seasoning.
4. Serve as soon as possible, topped with the nuts.

Serves 4–6
Preparation time: 15 minutes
Cooking time: About 5 minutes
Freezing: Not recommended

FIVE SPICE CHICKEN DRUMSTICKS

6 chicken drumsticks
FOR THE MARINADE:
2 tablespoons dark soy
* sauce*
1 tablespoon medium dry
* sherry*
1 clove garlic, crushed

1/2 teaspoon five spice
* powder*
1 teaspoon ground
* Szechwan peppercorns*
1 teaspoon sugar
TO GARNISH:
celery brushes
lime slices

Serves 6
Preparation time:
5 minutes, plus
marinating
Cooking time:
30–40 minutes
Freezing:
Recommended, at
end of stage 2

1. Mix the marinade ingredients together.
2. Place the drumsticks in a polythene bag, pour in the marinade and rub well to cover. Seal and chill overnight.
3. Turn onto a baking sheet and cook in a preheated oven, 180°C/350°F/Gas Mark 4, for 30–40 minutes, until brown.
4. Garnish with celery brushes and lime slices to serve.

CHICKEN AND FENNEL WITH LEMON AND GINGER

4 chicken quarters
2 tablespoons light soy
* sauce*
1 lemon
300 ml (1/2 pint) chicken
* stock*
1 teaspoon clear honey
2 teaspoons cornflour
2 tablespoons groundnut
* oil*

2 teaspoons sesame oil
2.5 cm (1 inch) cube fresh
* root ginger, cut into thin*
* sticks*
1 clove garlic, crushed
1 small bulb fennel, sliced
* lengthways*
fennel fronds to garnish

Serves 4
Preparation time:
10 minutes, plus
marinating
Cooking time:
15–20 minutes
Freezing:
Not recommended

1. Rub the chicken with the soy sauce and leave for 15 minutes.
2. Pare the rind from the lemon, then cut into very thin strips. Cut the lemon in half and squeeze the juice. Blend the juice with the stock, honey, cornflour and any soy sauce left after marinating the chicken. Set aside.
3. Heat the oils in a wok, add the chicken and cook for 2 minutes, turning, until browned all over. Remove and set aside.
4. Add the ginger, garlic and fennel to the wok and stir-fry for 2 minutes. Return the chicken with the lemon rind.
5. Pour in the blended stock, stir well, cover and simmer for 15–20 minutes or until the chicken is tender.
6. Garnish with fennel fronds to serve.

CHILLI CHICKEN WITH PEANUTS

This is a *hot* dish, so reduce the chillies if you prefer a milder strength. Removing the seeds helps cut down on the heat, too.

1 egg white
1 tablespoon light soy
    sauce
1 tablespoon dry sherry
1 tablespoon cornflour
350 g (12 oz) boneless
    chicken, diced
3 tablespoons groundnut
    oil
4 spring onions, sliced
    diagonally
1 clove garlic, crushed
1/2 red or green pepper,
    cored, seeded and diced

3–5 small dried red
    chillies, sliced
50 g (2 oz) unsalted
    peanuts
FOR THE SAUCE:
1 tablespoon soy sauce
1 teaspoon wine vinegar
1 teaspoon sugar
1 teaspoon cornflour
4–6 tablespoons light stock
    or water
salt and pepper to taste

Serves 3–6
Preparation time:
12 minutes
Cooking time:
6 minutes
Freezing:
Not recommended

1. Whisk the egg white with the soy sauce, sherry and cornflour. Add the chicken and mix well.
2. Mix the sauce ingredients together; set aside.
3. Heat the oil in a wok, add the chicken and stir-fry for about 3 minutes.
4. Add the spring onions, garlic, pepper and chillies and stir-fry for 2 minutes. Add the peanuts.
5. Pour in the sauce and cook, stirring, until thickened. Check the seasoning, transfer to a warmed serving dish and serve immediately.

CHICKEN AND BAMBOO SHOOTS
IN YELLOW BEAN SAUCE

2 tablespoons dry sherry
2 tablespoons light soy
    sauce
500 g (1 lb) boneless
    chicken breasts, cut into
    finger slices
6 dried Chinese
    mushrooms
1 teaspoon cornflour
2 tablespoons yellow bean
    sauce

3 tablespoons groundnut
    oil
6 spring onions, cut into
    strips
2 cloves garlic, crushed
230 g (8 oz) can bamboo
    shoots, drained and
    sliced
pinch of sugar
salt and pepper to taste

1. Place the sherry and soy sauce in a shallow dish, add the chicken and marinate for 30 minutes. Drain, reserving the marinade.

2. Soak the mushrooms in boiling water to cover for 20 minutes. Drain, reserving 4 tablespoons of the soaking liquid, discard the stalks and cut the caps into chunks.

3. Mix the marinade with the reserved soaking liquid, cornflour and bean sauce; set aside.

4. Heat the oil in a wok, add the chicken and stir-fry for 3–4 minutes.

5. Add the spring onions and garlic and stir-fry for 1 minute.

6. Add the sauce to the wok, stirring until thickened. Stir in the bamboo shoots, sugar, and salt and pepper. Transfer to a warmed serving dish and serve immediately.

Serves 3–4
Preparation time:
10 minutes,
plus soaking/
marinating time
Cooking time:
8 minutes
Freezing:
Not recommended

STIR-FRY DUCK WITH LEEKS

2 tablespoons dark soy
  sauce
2 dessertspoons plum
  sauce
pinch of five spice powder
  or ground cinnamon
2 tablespoons medium dry
  sherry
1 tablespoon wine vinegar
3 tablespoons stock or
  water
1 teaspoon cornflour

3 tablespoons groundnut
  oil
350 g (12 oz) duck breasts,
  skinned and sliced
  thinly
2 cloves garlic, crushed
4 spring onions, sliced
  diagonally
1 small red pepper, cored,
  seeded and sliced
2 leeks, sliced thinly
salt and pepper to taste

Serves 3–4
Preparation time:
10 minutes
Cooking time:
About 5 minutes
Freezing:
Not recommended

1. Blend together the soy sauce, plum sauce, spice, sherry, vinegar, stock or water and cornflour and set aside.
2. Heat 2 tablespoons of the oil in a wok, add the duck and stir-fry for 3 minutes. Season with salt and pepper, remove from the wok and set aside.
3. Heat the remaining oil in the wok, add the garlic, spring onions, red pepper and leeks and stir-fry for 2 minutes. Return the duck to the wok.
4. Add the blended sauce, stirring until thickened. Check the seasoning, transfer to a warmed serving dish and serve immediately.

DUCK WITH MANGETOUTS
AND CASHEWS

1 egg white
1 tablespoon cornflour
350 g (12 oz) duck breasts,
  skinned and cut into
  2.5 cm (1 inch) pieces
4 tablespoons groundnut
  oil
50 g (2 oz) unsalted
  cashew nuts
1 clove garlic, chopped
1 tablespoon fresh root
  ginger
5 spring onions, chopped
  roughly

3 celery sticks, sliced
  diagonally
125 g (4 oz) mangetouts,
  topped, tailed and
  halved
FOR THE SAUCE:
1 teaspoon cornflour
2 tablespoons dark soy
  sauce
1 teaspoon clear honey
2 tablespoons dry sherry
6 tablespoons water or
  stock
salt and pepper to taste

1. Whisk the egg white until frothy, then beat in the cornflour and a little salt and pepper. Add the duck and mix well.
2. Mix the sauce ingredients together in a cup.
3. Heat 1 tablespoon of the oil in a wok, add the cashew nuts and stir-fry for 30 seconds. Remove from the wok and set aside.
4. Heat the remaining oil, add the duck and stir-fry for 3 minutes. Remove with a slotted spoon and set aside.
5. Add the garlic, ginger, spring onions, celery and mangetouts to the wok and stir-fry for 2 minutes. Return the duck and cashews.
6. Pour in the sauce, stirring until thickened. Transfer to a warmed serving dish and serve as soon as possible.

Serves 3–4
Preparation time:
15 minutes
Cooking time:
6 minutes
Freezing:
Not recommended

RED COOKED DUCK WITH CORIANDER

'Red cooking' is characteristic of the Szechwan province of China, where food is served spicy hot to help combat the extremes of very cold winters and hot summers. It is not essential to this dish to use red food colouring, but it does add to the appearance.

2 kg (4¹/₂ lb) oven-ready duckling
1 onion
coriander stalks
FOR THE MARINADE:
1 teaspoon salt
2 teaspoons Szechwan peppercorns, roasted and coarsely ground
1 tablespoon grated fresh root ginger
1 teaspoon chilli oil
¹/₂ teaspoon five spice powder
pinch of ground cinnamon
2 tablespoons light soy sauce

2 cloves garlic, crushed
1 tablespoon medium dry sherry
3 spring onions, chopped finely
4 tablespoons chopped coriander leaves
2 teaspoons dark brown soft sugar
¹/₂ teaspoon red food colouring (optional)
TO COAT:
2 tablespoons clear honey
1 tablespoon sesame oil
TO GARNISH:
¹/₂ cucumber, sliced and shredded
coriander leaves

Serves 4
Preparation time: 10 minutes, plus marinating
Cooking time: 1¾ hours
Freezing: Recommended, at end of stage 2 only if fresh duckling used

1. Mix all the marinade ingredients together and spoon into a polythene bag.
2. Wipe the duck dry and prick the skin in several places. Stuff the body cavity with the onion and coriander stalks. Place the duck in the bag, rubbing the marinade in well. Leave in the refrigerator overnight.
3. Place the duck on a trivet in a roasting tin and scrape away any coriander sediment. Cook in a preheated oven, 180°C/350°F/Gas Mark 4, for about 1¾ hours, turning the bird over once or twice. Mix the honey and oil together and spread over the breast for the last 30 minutes, covering with foil if it starts to burn.
4. Garnish with cucumber and coriander and serve with plum sauce.

HONEY SOY TURKEY JOINTS

*3 tablespoons light soy
   sauce
2 tablespoons clear honey
1 tablespoon medium dry
   sherry
2 cloves garlic, crushed
1 tablespoon grated fresh
   root ginger*

*2 tablespoons sesame oil
1 tablespoon groundnut
   oil
1 kg (2 lb) turkey joints,
   e.g. wings, thighs,
   drumsticks
cucumber and shredded
   carrot to garnish*

1. Mix the soy sauce, honey, sherry, garlic and ginger together and set aside.
2. Heat the oils in a wok, add the turkey and stir-fry to brown. Add the sauce, stirring to coat the turkey. Cover and simmer for 20 minutes, shaking the wok occasionally.
3. Uncover and cook for 10 minutes, turning the joints to coat in the sauce. Transfer to a warmed serving dish and serve immediately, garnished with cucumber and carrot.

Serves 4–6
Preparation time:
5 minutes
Cooking time:
30 minutes
Freezing:
Not recommended

VENISON WITH WINTER VEGETABLES

Game recipes feature quite prominently in mainland China, the rich flavours marrying well with classic Chinese flavourings. This is an Anglicized adaptation of one.

5 tablespoons medium dry sherry	300 ml (1/2 pint) stock or water
5 tablespoons dark soy sauce	2 teaspoons cornflour
1 tablespoon each hoisin sauce, plum sauce and wine vinegar	3 tablespoons groundnut oil
1 tablespoon grated fresh root ginger	4 spring onions, sliced
	3 carrots, cut into strips
4 venison cutlets, each weighing 175 g (6 oz)	1 parsnip, cut into strips
	2 celery sticks, sliced diagonally
	celery leaves to garnish

Serves 4
Preparation time: 10 minutes, plus marinating
Cooking time: 15–20 minutes
Freezing: Recommended, at end of stage 1

1. Mix the sherry, soy, hoisin and plum sauces, vinegar and ginger together, then rub well into the cutlets. Cover and marinate for at least 2 hours, preferably overnight. Drain, reserving the marinade.
2. Blend the marinade with the stock or water and cornflour; set aside.
3. Heat the oil in a wok, add the venison and cook for 1 minute on each side. Remove and set aside.
4. Add the vegetables to the wok and stir-fry for 2 minutes. Stir in the blended stock until thickened.
5. Return the cutlets to the wok, spoon over some of the sauce, cover and simmer for 15–20 minutes, turning once, until tender. Garnish with celery leaves to serve.

BRAISED RABBIT WITH SPINACH

4 dried Chinese mushrooms	6 rabbit portions
1 egg white	6 spring onions, sliced diagonally
2 1/2 tablespoons cornflour	2 cloves garlic, crushed
150 ml (1/4 pint) stock or water	75 g (3 oz) ham, chopped
1 tablespoon light soy sauce	salt and pepper to taste
	TO SERVE:
1 tablespoon hoisin sauce	500 g (1 lb) spinach, steamed
2 tablespoons dry sherry	spring onion brushes (optional)
150 ml (1/4 pint) groundnut oil	

1. Soak the mushrooms in boiling water to cover for 20 minutes. Drain, reserving the liquid; make up to 150 ml (¼ pint). Discard the stalks and slice the caps; set aside.
2. Beat the egg white until frothy, then beat in 2 tablespoons of the cornflour and a pinch of salt.
3. Blend the stock or water, reserved soaking liquid, soy and hoisin sauces, sherry and remaining cornflour together; set aside.
4. Heat the oil in a wok, dip the rabbit portions in the egg white batter, then fry quickly on both sides until browned. Remove with a slotted spoon and set aside.
5. Pour off all but 1 tablespoon oil from the wok. Add the spring onions, garlic and ham; stir-fry for 2 minutes. Pour in the blended stock and cook, stirring, until thickened.
6. Return the rabbit to the wok with the mushrooms, cover and simmer for about 25 minutes, until tender, turning once. Check the seasoning.
7. Arrange the spinach around a warmed serving dish and spoon the rabbit and sauce into the centre. Garnish with spring onion brushes, if you wish, to serve.

Serves 3–6
Preparation time: 15 minutes, plus soaking time
Cooking time: About 25 minutes
Freezing: Not recommended

RICE & NOODLES

The two staple foods of Chinese people worldwide, rice and noodles, can now be bought in an increasing variety in this country.

Long-grain Patna-type rice, white or brown, is the most common. The latter takes nearly three times as long to cook, but contains more vitamins and dietary fibre and has a delicious nutty taste. Another variety is Chinese sticky (or glutinous) rice—this has a shorter grain which cooks to a slight stickiness, ideal for handling with chopsticks as the grains form into a soft mound when lightly pressed together.

Chinese noodles are sold in an almost bewildering variety and can be made from wheat, buckwheat and rice flours—even ground mung beans. Although I have specified some noodle varieties, the types of noodle are in fact interchangeable. Follow individual packet instructions for cooking.

EGG FOO YUNG RICE

2 eggs, beaten
3 tablespoons groundnut oil
4 spring onions, sliced
1 clove garlic, crushed
1 tablespoon grated fresh root ginger
1/2 green pepper, cored, seeded and cut into diamond shapes
2 celery sticks, sliced diagonally
125 g (4 oz) bean sprouts, preferably home-sprouted
2 tablespoons light soy sauce
2 tablespoons dry sherry
2 teaspoons sesame oil
250 g (8 oz) long-grain white or brown rice, cooked
salt and pepper to taste

Serves 3–4
Preparation time: 10 minutes, plus cooking rice
Cooking time: 6 minutes
Freezing: Not recommended

1. Season the eggs with salt and pepper. Heat 1 tablespoon of the oil in a small pan and lightly scramble the eggs, until just firm but still a little creamy. Set aside.
2. Heat the remaining oil in a wok, add the spring onions, garlic, ginger, green pepper and celery and stir-fry for 2–3 minutes.
3. Add the bean sprouts and stir-fry for 1 minute, then add the soy sauce, sherry, sesame oil, and salt and pepper.
4. Add the rice, toss well and reheat. Fork through the eggs, transfer to a warmed serving dish and serve immediately.

Illustrated top right: Vegetable and Nut Fried Rice (page 50)

SESAME SEED RICE

Perfectly cooked plain rice is an ideal accompaniment to all Chinese dishes, particularly with a simple but very tasty dressing. There are two easy methods of cooking rice.

250 g (8 oz) long-grain white or brown rice, or Chinese sticky rice

2 tablespoons sesame seeds
2 tablespoons sesame oil
salt to taste

Serves 4
Preparation time: 1 minute
Cooking time: White rice: 11 or 20 minutes; brown rice: 30 or 40 minutes
Freezing: Not recommended

Method 1. Cook the rice in plenty of lightly salted boiling water, 11 minutes for white rice, 30 minutes for brown rice. Drain and rinse under hot water.

Method 2. Pour the rice into a measuring jug to ascertain its volume. Place in a pan. Measure twice the quantity of cold water and add to the pan with salt, if you wish. Bring to the boil, cover and simmer gently, 20 minutes for white rice, about 40 minutes for brown, until the water is absorbed and the rice tender; do not lift the lid until near the end of the cooking time—brown rice may need a little extra water. Do not drain, but fork through.

To serve. Fry the sesame seeds in the oil for about 30 seconds. Toss immediately into the rice and serve as soon as possible.

VEGETABLE AND NUT FRIED RICE

2 tablespoons groundnut oil
1 leek, sliced thinly
2 carrots, sliced thinly
1 clove garlic, crushed
1 tablespoon grated fresh root ginger
75 g (3 oz) baby corn cobs, halved
75 g (3 oz) button mushrooms, halved

50 g (2 oz) mangetouts, topped and halved
250 g (8 oz) long-grain white or brown rice, cooked
3 tablespoons light soy sauce
2 teaspoons sesame oil
50 g (2 oz) unsalted cashew nuts, toasted
salt and pepper to taste

Serves 4
Preparation time: 10 minutes, plus cooking rice
Cooking time: 5 minutes
Freezing: Not recommended

Illustrated on page 49

1. Heat the oil in a wok, add the leek, carrots, garlic and ginger and stir-fry for 2 minutes.
2. Add the corn, mushrooms and mangetouts and stir-fry for 1 minute.
3. Toss in the rice, soy sauce, sesame oil, and salt and pepper, and stir-fry until heated through.
4. Sprinkle with the nuts and serve immediately.

FRIED RICE WITH CUCUMBER AND CORIANDER

¹/₄ cucumber
2–3 tablespoons
    groundnut oil
3 spring onions, sliced
2 teaspoons grated fresh
    root ginger

1 clove garlic, crushed
250 g (8 oz) long-grain or
    sticky rice, cooked
2 tablespoons chopped
    coriander leaves
salt and pepper to taste

1. Cut the cucumber into 2 mm (⅛ inch) slices, then cut the slices into shreds.
2. Heat 2 tablespoons oil in a wok, add the spring onions, ginger, garlic and cucumber, and stir-fry for 2 minutes.
3. Add the rice and extra oil, if necessary, and stir-fry until heated through. Add the coriander leaves, and salt and pepper, and toss well. Transfer to a warmed serving dish and serve immediately.

Serves 2–3
Preparation time:
6 minutes, plus cooking rice
Cooking time:
4 minutes
Freezing:
Not recommended

CHICKEN RICE WITH DRIED SHRIMPS

25 g (1 oz) dried shrimps
3 tablespoons groundnut oil
3 spring onions, sliced diagonally
1 tablespoon grated fresh root ginger
1 clove garlic, crushed
175 g (6 oz) cooked chicken, shredded (approximately)
50 g (2 oz) frozen peas

125 g (4 oz) bean sprouts
¼ small crisp lettuce, shredded
175 g (6 oz) long-grain white or brown rice, cooked
2 tablespoons light soy or oyster sauce
few drops chilli oil (optional)
½ teaspoon sugar
salt and pepper to taste

Serves 4
Preparation time:
10 minutes, plus cooking rice and soaking time
Cooking time:
7 minutes
Freezing:
Not recommended

1. Soak the shrimps in a little warm water to cover for 15 minutes. Drain, reserving the water.
2. Heat the oil in a wok, add the spring onions, ginger and garlic and stir-fry for 1 minute.
3. Add the chicken, shrimps and peas and stir-fry for 2 minutes. Toss in the bean sprouts and lettuce.
4. Add the rice, soy or oyster sauce, reserved shrimp water, chilli oil, if using, sugar, and salt and pepper. Heat through, tossing well together. Transfer to a warmed serving dish and serve immediately.

NOODLES WITH HOT BEAN PASTE

This is a fiery noodle dish—perfect for winter evenings. If you're not sure how hot your guests like their food, serve the hot bean chilli paste separately, to be mixed in according to taste. It is well worth sprouting your own beans —use them while the sprouts are still short.

175 g (6 oz) instant rice or egg noodles
1 tablespoon sesame oil
2 tablespoons dark soy sauce
2 tablespoons medium dry sherry
2 teaspoons cornflour
2 tablespoons groundnut oil
2 leeks, sliced thinly, diagonally

1 clove garlic, crushed
1 tablespoon chopped fresh root ginger
125 g (4 oz) bean sprouts (preferably short-sprouted)
450 ml (¾ pint) chicken stock
2–3 tablespoons hot bean chilli paste
salt and pepper to taste

1. Soak the noodles according to packet instructions. Drain, toss in the sesame oil, then arrange on a serving dish and keep warm.

2. Blend the soy sauce, sherry and cornflour together.

3. Heat the groundnut oil in a wok, add the leeks, garlic, ginger and bean sprouts and stir-fry for 2 minutes. Add the blended sauce and stock and bring to the boil. Simmer for 1 minute, then stir in the bean paste. Check the seasoning and spoon over the noodles to serve.

Serves 4–6
Preparation time:
5 minutes, plus soaking time
Cooking time:
5 minutes
Freezing:
Not recommended

CHILLI NOODLES WITH CHINESE CHIVES

All you need for cooking this dish is a kettle. Chinese (or garlic) chives are garlic-flavoured chives with attractive white flower heads—easy to grow in this country. Alternatively, chop ordinary chives with a clove of garlic.

250 g (8 oz) instant rice or egg noodles
2 cloves garlic, crushed
2 teaspoons grated fresh root ginger
1 teaspoon chilli oil
1 tablespoon sesame oil

1–2 teaspoons roughly crushed Szechwan peppercorns
1 teaspoon five spice powder
3 tablespoons coarsely chopped Chinese chives
salt to taste

Serves 4–6
Preparation time:
2 minutes, plus soaking time
Freezing:
Not recommended

1. Soak the noodles according to packet instructions, drain and salt lightly.
2. Toss in the remaining ingredients, reserving 1 tablespoon chives. Sprinkle these chives on top of the noodles and serve immediately.

NOODLES WITH SHRIMP AND LETTUCE

2 tablespoons dried shrimps
2 tablespoons oyster sauce
1 teaspoon cornflour
175 g (6 oz) instant rice noodles

2 tablespoons groundnut oil
3 spring onions, sliced
1 clove garlic, crushed
1/2 small crisp lettuce, shredded
salt and pepper to taste

Serves 3–4
Preparation time:
7 minutes, plus soaking time
Cooking time:
4 minutes
Freezing:
Not recommended

1. Soak the shrimps in 150 ml (1/4 pint) warm water for 15 minutes. Drain, reserving the soaking liquid, and set aside.
2. Blend the reserved liquid, oyster sauce and cornflour together and set aside.
3. Soak the noodles according to packet instructions.
4. Heat the oil in a wok, add the spring onions, garlic and shrimps and stir-fry for 1 minute. Add the lettuce and stir-fry for 1 minute.
5. Pour in the blended liquid and cook, stirring, until thickened. Stir in the noodles, and salt and pepper. Transfer to a warmed serving dish and serve immediately.

NOODLES WITH TOFU AND CASHEWS

4 dried Chinese
   mushrooms
175 g (6 oz) rice noodles
2 teaspoons sesame oil
2 tablespoons light soy
   sauce
1 teaspoon cornflour
3 tablespoons groundnut
   oil
125 g (4 oz) tofu, cut into
   2 cm (³/4 inch) cubes

75 g (3 oz) unsalted
   cashew nuts
3 spring onions, sliced
1 clove garlic, crushed
1 tablespoon chopped fresh
   root ginger
125 g (4 oz) bean sprouts
   (preferably short or
   home-sprouted)
salt and pepper to taste

Serves 3–4
Preparation time:
5 minutes, plus
soaking time
Cooking time:
7 minutes
Freezing:
Not recommended

1. Soak the mushrooms in boiling water to cover for 20 minutes. Drain, reserving 150 ml (¼ pint) of the water. Discard the stalks and slice the caps.

2. Soak the noodles according to packet instructions. Drain, season with salt and pepper and toss in the sesame oil. Place in a warmed serving dish.

3. Blend the soy sauce, reserved mushroom liquid, cornflour, and salt and pepper together and set aside.

4. Heat half of the groundnut oil in a wok, add the tofu and stir-fry for 2 minutes, until browned. Remove and set aside.

5. Add the cashew nuts and stir-fry for 30 seconds, until lightly browned. Remove and set aside.

6. Heat the remaining oil, add the spring onions, garlic, ginger and bean sprouts and stir-fry for 2 minutes. Pour in the blended stock and cook, stirring, until thickened.

7. Return the tofu and cashews to the wok and check the seasoning. Spoon onto the noodles and serve.

CHOW MEIN

125 g (4 oz) Chinese egg
   noodles
2 teaspoons sesame oil
3 tablespoons groundnut
   oil
4 spring onions, sliced
1 clove garlic, crushed
2 carrots, cut into sticks
7.5 cm (3 inch) piece
   cucumber, cut into sticks
125 g (4 oz) thin green
   beans, halved

125 g (4 oz) button
   mushrooms, quartered
125 g (4 oz) bean sprouts
   (preferably short-
   sprouted mung beans)
300 ml (½ pint) chicken
   stock
2 tablespoons dark soy
   sauce
1 tablespoon cornflour
2 eggs, beaten
salt, pepper and sugar

1. Cook the noodles according to packet instructions, drain and toss in the sesame oil. Set aside.

2. Heat 2 tablespoons of the groundnut oil in a wok, add the spring onions, garlic, carrots, cucumber and beans and stir-fry for 2 minutes. Add the mushrooms and bean sprouts and stir-fry for 1 minute.

3. Add the stock, salt, pepper and a pinch of sugar, then cover and simmer for 2 minutes.

4. Blend the soy sauce and cornflour with a little water, stir into the vegetables and bring to a good simmer. Toss in the noodles and transfer to a warmed serving dish.

5. Heat the remaining oil in a small frying pan and make a flat soft omelette with the eggs, lightly scrambling it. Stir into the chow mein and serve immediately.

Serves 4
Preparation time:
12 minutes
Cooking time:
12–15 minutes
Freezing:
Not recommended

VEGETABLE & VEGETARIAN DISHES

Most of these dishes can be served to accompany meat and fish. If you wish to serve a vegetarian meal, serve two of the more substantial dishes which contain no meat or fish and accompany with rice or noodles. Such a combination produces a tasty, attractive and healthy meal. Use a vegetable stock.

BABY CORN WITH MANGETOUTS

1 tablespoon groundnut oil
1 tablespoon sesame oil
350 g (12 oz) baby corn cobs
125 g (4 oz) mangetouts, topped and tailed
2 spring onions, cut into 2.5 cm (1 inch) lengths
2 tablespoons light soy sauce
salt and pepper to taste

Serves 3–6
Preparation time:
2 minutes
Cooking time:
3 minutes
Freezing:
Not recommended

1. Heat the oils in a wok, add the corn cobs, mangetouts and spring onions and stir-fry for 3 minutes. Add the soy sauce, and salt and pepper.
2. Transfer to a warmed serving dish to serve.

WHITE RADISH WITH RED PEPPER AND BLACK BEANS

White radish (mooli) is a long white milder version of our familiar red radish. Its mild flavour and crunchy texture combine well with red pepper and black beans.

2 tablespoons groundnut oil
350 g (12 oz) white radish, peeled, halved lengthways, then sliced diagonally
1 red pepper, cored, seeded and sliced
4 spring onions, sliced
1 clove garlic, crushed
1 tablespoon chopped fresh root ginger
1½ tablespoons salted black beans, soaked if packeted
1 teaspoon sesame oil

Serves 3–4
Preparation time:
10 minutes
Cooking time:
2 minutes
Freezing:
Not recommended

1. Heat the groundnut oil in a wok, add the radish, red pepper, spring onions, garlic and ginger and stir-fry for 2 minutes.
2. Stir in the black beans and trickle over the sesame oil. Toss well, transfer to a warmed serving dish and serve immediately.

BROCCOLI WITH MUSHROOMS

*250 g (8 oz) broccoli
    florets
1 tablespoon groundnut
    oil
1 tablespoon sesame oil*

*3 spring onions, sliced
125 g (4 oz) button
    mushrooms, sliced
2 tablespoons oyster sauce*

Serves 3–4
Preparation time:
5 minutes
Cooking time:
2–3 minutes
Freezing:
Not recommended

1. Slice the broccoli florets into bite-size pieces.
2. Heat the oils in a wok, add the broccoli, spring onions and mushrooms and stir-fry for 2–3 minutes.
3. Add the oyster sauce and toss well. Transfer to a warmed serving dish and serve immediately.

BROCCOLI AND CAULIFLOWER WITH CHILLI AND ALMONDS

For a vegetarian dish, omit the dried shrimps.

*2 tablespoons dried
    shrimps
1 tablespoon dark soy
    sauce
1 teaspoon cornflour
2 tablespoons groundnut
    oil
25 g (1 oz) blanched
    almonds, halved
4 spring onions, sliced*

*1 large red chilli, seeded
    and sliced
1 clove garlic, crushed
1 tablespoon shredded
    fresh root ginger
1/2 small cauliflower,
    broken into small florets
250 g (8 oz) broccoli,
    broken into small florets
pepper to taste*

Serves 4–6
Preparation time:
10 minutes, plus
soaking time
Cooking time:
6 minutes
Freezing:
Not recommended

1. Soak the shrimps in 6 tablespoons warm water for 15 minutes. Drain, reserving the water, and set aside.
2. Blend the reserved water, soy sauce and cornflour together and set aside.
3. Heat half of the oil in a wok, add the almonds and stir-fry until just browned. Remove and set aside.
4. Heat the remaining oil in the wok, add the shrimps, spring onions, chilli, garlic and ginger and stir-fry for 1 minute.
5. Add the cauliflower and broccoli and stir-fry for 2 minutes. Pour in the blended sauce, stirring; cover and simmer for 2 minutes. Check the seasoning.
6. Transfer to a warmed serving dish, sprinkle with the almonds and serve immediately.

HOT PEPPER SPINACH WITH GARLIC

*2 tablespoons groundnut
    oil
1 tablespoon sesame oil
3 cloves garlic, halved*

*500 g (1 lb) spinach
1 dessertspoon crushed
    Szechwan peppercorns
salt to taste*

1. Place the oils and garlic in a wok and heat gently for about 2 minutes; do not allow to burn. Discard the garlic.
2. Increase the heat and stir-fry the spinach, adding it in batches—take care, it will spit.
3. Season with the peppercorns and salt, transfer to a warmed serving dish and serve immediately.

**Serves 3—4
Preparation time:**
5 minutes
Cooking time:
5 minutes
Freezing:
Not recommended

GINGER-STEAMED ASPARAGUS AND CARROT

Use the tasty stock left after cooking the asparagus for another dish.

350 g (12 oz) asparagus
3 carrots
600 ml (1 pint) chicken stock
1 clove garlic, halved

4 thin slices fresh root ginger
1 onion, sliced
2 teaspoons sesame oil
salt and pepper to taste

Serves 3–6
Preparation time:
7 minutes
Cooking time:
6 minutes
Freezing:
Not recommended

1. Cut the woody stems from the asparagus, then cut into 5 cm (2 inch) lengths. Set the tips aside.
2. Cut the carrots into strips the same length.
3. Place the stock, garlic, ginger and onion in the base of a steamer and bring to the boil.
4. Steam the asparagus stalks and carrots for 4 minutes. Add the tips, season with salt and pepper and steam for 2 minutes.
5. Toss the vegetables in the oil, transfer to a warmed serving dish and serve immediately.

BABY CORN WITH MUSHROOMS AND LEEKS

3 dried Chinese mushrooms
2 tablespoons groundnut oil
2 leeks, sliced thinly, diagonally
2 cloves garlic, crushed
175 g (6 oz) baby corn cobs

125 g (4 oz) button mushrooms
2 tablespoons dark soy sauce
2 tablespoons medium dry sherry
1 teaspoon cornflour
salt and pepper to taste

Serves 3–4
Preparation time:
5 minutes, plus soaking time
Cooking time:
5 minutes
Freezing:
Not recommended

1. Soak the mushrooms in boiling water to cover for 20 minutes. Drain, reserving 150 ml (¼ pint) of the water, discard the stalks and slice the caps; set aside.
2. Heat the oil in a wok, add the leeks and garlic and stir-fry for 1 minute. Add the Chinese mushrooms, corn cobs and button mushrooms and stir-fry for 2 minutes.
3. Blend the soy sauce, sherry, reserved soaking liquid and cornflour together and pour into the vegetables, stirring until thickened. Season with salt and pepper. Transfer to a warmed serving dish and serve immediately.

CASHEW AND SWEET PEPPER DUMPLINGS

These are best cooked in a stacking steamer, unless you wish to cook and serve them in two batches. The filling can be prepared beforehand, but the dough is best made just before you cook.

250 g (8 oz) self-raising flour
½ teaspoon salt
150 ml (¼ pint) water (approximately)
FOR THE FILLING:
3 dried Chinese mushrooms
2 tablespoons groundnut oil
2 teaspoons sesame oil
3 spring onions, chopped
1 clove garlic, crushed

1 small red pepper, cored, seeded and chopped finely
125 g (4 oz) button mushrooms, chopped finely
50 g (2 oz) unsalted cashew nuts, toasted and chopped
2 tablespoons chopped coriander leaves
2 tablespoons dark soy sauce

Serves 4–8
Preparation time:
25 minutes, plus soaking time
Cooking time:
About 25 minutes
Freezing:
Not recommended

1. First, prepare the filling. Soak the mushrooms in boiling water to cover for 20 minutes. Drain, discard the stalks and chop the caps.

2. Heat the oils in a wok, add the mushroom caps, spring onions, garlic, pepper and button mushrooms and stir-fry for 3 minutes. Add the cashews, coriander leaves and soy sauce. Set aside.

3. Sift the flour and salt into a bowl, then add enough water to mix to a soft but firm dough. Divide into 16 small balls, then roll out thinly on a lightly floured board to 7.5 cm (3 inch) rounds.

4. Brush the edges with water, spoon in a sixteenth of the filling, then draw up the edges to form a pouch. Press well to seal. Repeat with the remaining dough and filling to make 16 dumplings.

5. Place on a greased steamer base and steam for about 25 minutes. Transfer to a warmed serving dish and serve with Sesame Chilli Sauce (below), Ginger Soy Sauce or Barbecue Plum Sauce (page 31), or bought sauces such as yellow bean, plum, lemon and ginger, hoisin.

Sesame Chilli Sauce. Mix together 3 tablespoons light soy sauce, 1 tablespoon sesame oil, ¼ teaspoon five spice powder, 1 small crushed dried chilli, and 1 finely chopped spring onion.

MYRIAD OF STIR-FRY PEPPERS

For a vegetarian dish, omit the ham.

2 tablespoons groundnut oil
1 each green, red and yellow pepper, cored, seeded and sliced
2 cloves garlic, crushed
1 green or red chilli, seeded and sliced
3 spring onions, sliced diagonally
2 slices ham, shredded
1 tablespoon light soy sauce
2 tablespoons medium dry sherry
1 teaspoon sugar

1. Heat the oil in a wok, add the peppers and stir-fry for 2 minutes.
2. Add the garlic, chilli, spring onions and ham and stir-fry for 1 minute.
3. Sprinkle in the soy sauce, sherry and sugar and cook, stirring, for 1 minute. Transfer to a warmed serving dish and serve immediately.

Serves 3–4
Preparation time: 10 minutes
Cooking time: 4 minutes
Freezing: Not recommended

STIR-FRIED TOMATO OMELETTE

A quick recipe to serve as part of a main vegetarian meal or as an accompanying side dish.

*⅓ cucumber, sliced thinly,
    then shredded
3 eggs
1 tablespoon light soy
    sauce
1 tablespoon sesame oil
1 tablespoon groundnut
    oil*

*2 spring onions, sliced
    thinly
1 clove garlic, crushed
2 tomatoes, seeded and cut
    into strips
salt and pepper to taste*

Serves 2–3
Preparation time:
10 minutes
Cooking time:
4 minutes
Freezing:
Not recommended

1. Arrange the cucumber around a serving plate.
2. Beat the eggs with the soy sauce and a little salt and pepper.
3. Heat the oils in a wok, add the spring onions, garlic and tomatoes and stir-fry for about 2 minutes.
4. Pour in the eggs and cook lightly, stirring occasionally so that you get a texture like a scrambled omelette—don't overstir or overcook. Spoon onto the prepared plate and serve immediately.

AUBERGINE WITH DRIED MUSHROOMS AND OYSTER SAUCE

*4 dried Chinese
    mushrooms
3 tablespoons groundnut
    oil
3 spring onions, sliced
    diagonally
1 aubergine, sliced thinly*

*1 clove garlic, crushed
2 tablespoons oyster sauce
1 teaspoon cornflour
2 teaspoons chopped
    coriander leaves
salt and pepper to taste*

Serves 3–4
Preparation time:
5 minutes, plus
soaking time
Cooking time:
5 minutes
Freezing:
Not recommended

1. Soak the mushrooms in boiling water to cover for 20 minutes. Drain, reserving 150 ml (¼ pint) of the water, discard the stalks, slice the caps and set aside.
2. Heat the oil in a wok, add the spring onions, aubergine, mushroom caps and garlic and stir-fry for 2 minutes.
3. Blend the reserved soaking liquid with the oyster sauce and cornflour, pour into the wok and stir until thickened. Cover and simmer for 2 minutes. Season with salt and pepper.
4. Transfer to a warmed serving dish and sprinkle with the coriander leaves.

CHINESE LEAF WITH CHESTNUTS AND BACON

20 dried chestnuts
3 dried Chinese
mushrooms
1 tablespoon medium dry
sherry
2 tablespoons light soy
sauce
½ teaspoon caster sugar
2 teaspoons cornflour

1 tablespoon groundnut
oil
6 rashers tendersweet
streaky bacon, derinded
and diced
6 spring onions, sliced
1 clove garlic, crushed
½ head Chinese leaf, cut
into chunks
pepper to taste

Serves 3–4
Preparation time:
10 minutes, plus
soaking time
Cooking time:
6 minutes
Freezing:
Not recommended

1. Soak the chestnuts and mushrooms together in boiling water to cover for 30 minutes. Drain, reserving 2 tablespoons of the water.
2. Discard the mushroom stalks. Chop the mushroom caps and chestnuts roughly.
3. Mix the sherry, soy sauce, sugar, cornflour and pepper with the reserved water and set aside.
4. Heat the oil in a wok, add the bacon and stir-fry for 2 minutes. Remove with a slotted spoon and set aside.
5. Add the spring onions and garlic to the wok and stir-fry for 1 minute, then stir in the Chinese leaf, chestnuts and mushrooms. Cover and simmer for 2 minutes.
6. Return the bacon to the wok, pour in the blended sauce and toss well. Serve immediately.

RED-COOKED TOFU WITH MUSHROOMS AND LETTUCE

250 g (8 oz) tofu or bean
curd, cut into 2.5 cm
(1 inch) cubes
4 dried Chinese
mushrooms
1 teaspoon cornflour
2 tablespoons groundnut
oil
3 spring onions, sliced
FOR THE MARINADE:
3 tablespoons dark soy
sauce
2 tablespoons medium dry
sherry

2 teaspoons dark brown
soft sugar
1 clove garlic, crushed
1 tablespoon grated fresh
root ginger
½ teaspoon five spice
powder
Szechwan peppercorns,
roasted and ground, to
taste
TO SERVE:
¼ head Chinese leaf,
shredded
1 spring onion, shredded

1. Mix the marinade ingredients together, add the tofu or bean curd, toss well and leave to marinate for 20 minutes. Drain, reserving the marinade, and set aside.

2. Soak the mushrooms in boiling water to cover for 20 minutes. Drain, reserving the water, discard the stalks and slice the caps; set aside.

3. Blend 6 tablespoons of the soaking liquid with the cornflour and reserved marinade and set aside.

4. Heat the oil in a wok, add the tofu or bean curd and stir-fry for 1 minute, until browned. Remove and set aside.

5. Add the spring onions and mushrooms to the wok and stir-fry for 1 minute. Pour in the marinade mixture, stirring until thickened, return the tofu or bean curd and simmer for 1 minute.

6. Transfer to a warmed serving dish, lined with the Chinese leaf and spring onion.

Serves 3–4
Preparation time:
10 minutes, plus soaking time
Cooking time:
5 minutes
Freezing:
Not recommended

BROAD BEANS AND MUSHROOMS

6 tablespoons chicken or
   vegetable stock
1 teaspoon cornflour
2 tablespoons groundnut
   oil
3 spring onions, sliced
   diagonally
2 teaspoons chopped fresh
   root ginger

2 cloves garlic, crushed
125 g (4 oz) button
   mushrooms, sliced
250 g (8 oz) shelled broad
   beans
2 tablespoons chopped
   coriander leaves
salt and ground Szechwan
   peppercorns to taste

Serves 3–4
Preparation time:
5 minutes
Cooking time:
7 minutes
Freezing:
Not recommended

1. Blend the stock with the cornflour and set aside.
2. Heat the oil in a wok, add the spring onions, ginger and garlic and stir-fry for 1 minute. Add the mushrooms and stir-fry for 2 minutes.
3. Stir in the blended stock until thickened, add the beans, and salt and ground peppercorns, cover and simmer for 3 minutes, shaking the wok occasionally.
4. Stir in the coriander leaves, transfer to a warmed serving dish and serve immediately.

SPINACH WITH TOFU

125 g (4 oz) tofu or bean
   curd, cut into 2 cm
   (¾ inch) cubes
2 tablespoons dark soy
   sauce
3 tablespoons groundnut
   oil
3 spring onions, cut into
   strips

1 teaspoon chopped fresh
   root ginger
350 g (12 oz) spinach
227 g (8 oz) can bamboo
   shoots, drained
salt, pepper and sugar to
   taste
2 teaspoons sesame seeds,
   toasted, to serve

Serves 3
Preparation time:
10 minutes
Cooking time:
7 minutes
Freezing:
Not recommended

1. Toss the tofu or bean curd in the soy sauce and leave to marinate for 5 minutes. Drain, reserving the sauce.
2. Heat the oil in a wok, add the tofu or bean curd and stir-fry for 2 minutes. Remove and set aside.
3. Add the spring onions and ginger to the wok and stir-fry for 1 minute.
4. Add the spinach in batches, tossing well until wilted. Add the bamboo shoots and stir-fry for 30 seconds. Pour in the reserved soy sauce, season with salt, pepper and a good pinch of sugar, and add the tofu or bean curd.
5. Transfer to a warmed serving dish, scatter with the sesame seeds and serve immediately.

SWEET AND SOUR MIXED VEGETABLES

The vegetables listed here are only a suggestion—vary them according to preference and availability.

3 tablespoons groundnut oil
2 leeks, sliced diagonally
1 clove garlic, crushed
1 dessertspoon chopped fresh root ginger
2 celery sticks, sliced diagonally
1 small red pepper, cored, seeded and sliced
3 carrots, sliced thinly
2 courgettes or ⅓ cucumber, sliced

125 g (4 oz) broccoli florets, sliced if large
FOR THE SAUCE:
3 tablespoons soy sauce
3 tablespoons wine vinegar
3 tablespoons medium dry sherry
1 tablespoon clear honey
2 tablespoons light brown soft sugar
90–125 ml (3–4 fl oz) water
1 teaspoon cornflour

Serves 4–6
Preparation time:
12 minutes
Cooking time:
5 minutes
Freezing:
Not recommended

1. Mix all the sauce ingredients together and set aside.
2. Heat the oil in a wok, add the remaining ingredients and stir-fry for 2 minutes.
3. Pour in the sauce, stirring until thickened, cover and cook for 2 minutes. Transfer to a warmed serving dish and serve as soon as possible.

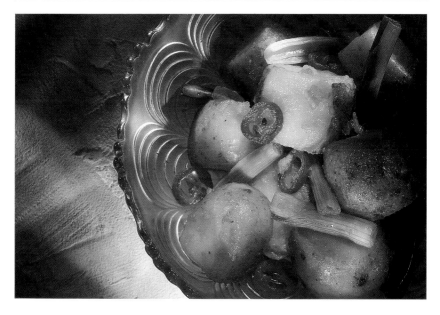

GARLIC POTATOES WITH CHILLI

A delicious alternative to rice or noodles. This dish is best made with freshly boiled potatoes, but cold cooked potatoes would also be suitable.

500 g (1 lb) potatoes, scrubbed and cut into 2.5 cm (1 inch) cubes
3 spring onions
2 tablespoons groundnut oil

1–2 red chillies, seeded and sliced
3 cloves garlic, crushed
2 tablespoons light soy sauce
1 tablespoon sesame oil
salt to taste

1. Boil the potatoes in lightly salted water for about 10 minutes, until just tender—do not overcook. Drain and set aside.
2. Meanwhile, cut the spring onions into 3.5 cm (1½ inch) lengths, separating the white and green parts. Quarter the white bulbs.
3. Heat the groundnut oil in a wok, add the potatoes and stir-fry for 2 minutes, until lightly browned.
4. Add the white part of the spring onions, chillies and garlic and stir-fry for 1 minute.
5. Add the soy sauce, sesame oil and green part of the spring onions and stir-fry over the heat for 30 seconds. Transfer to a warmed serving dish and serve immediately.

Serves 3–4
Preparation time: 10 minutes
Cooking time: 14 minutes
Freezing: Not recommended

BAMBOO SHOOTS AND
GREEN BEANS IN YELLOW BEAN SAUCE

2 tablespoons groundnut oil	*125 g (4 oz) button mushrooms, halved*
1 leek, sliced thinly	*2 tablespoons yellow bean sauce*
1 clove garlic, crushed	
1 teaspoon grated fresh root ginger	*150 ml (¼ pint) light stock or water*
250 g (8 oz) green beans, sliced diagonally	*227 g (8 oz) can bamboo shoots, drained*
	pepper to taste

Serves 3–4
Preparation time: 7 minutes
Cooking time: 5–6 minutes
Freezing: Not recommended

1. Heat the oil in a wok, add the leek, garlic, ginger and beans and stir-fry for 2 minutes.
2. Add the mushrooms and stir-fry for 1 minute. Stir in the yellow bean sauce, stock or water, bamboo shoots and pepper, then cover and simmer for 2–3 minutes. Transfer to a warmed serving dish and serve immediately.

CARROT, FENNEL AND PEPPER STIR-FRY

This dish makes a good accompaniment to fish dishes. It could also form part of a vegetarian meal.

1 teaspoon five spice powder	*3 tablespoons groundnut oil*
2 tablespoons light soy sauce	*4 spring onions, cut into 2.5 cm (1 inch) lengths*
150 ml (¼ pint) light stock or water	*1 clove garlic*
	3 carrots, sliced thinly
1 teaspoon cornflour	*1 bulb fennel, sliced thinly*
2 teaspoons wine vinegar	*1 green pepper, cored, seeded and sliced thinly*
	salt and pepper to taste

Serves 3–4
Preparation time: 6 minutes
Cooking time: 6 minutes
Freezing: Not recommended

1. Blend the five spice powder, soy sauce, stock or water, cornflour and vinegar together. Set aside.
2. Heat the oil in a wok, add the spring onions, garlic and vegetables and stir-fry for 2 minutes.
3. Add the blended sauce, stirring until thickened, cover and simmer for 2–3 minutes, shaking the wok occasionally. Check the seasoning and transfer to a warmed serving dish. Serve immediately.

HOT SHREDDED CUCUMBER AND LETTUCE

*2 tablespoons light soy
    sauce*
*1 tablespoon medium dry
    sherry*
*4 tablespoons light stock or
    water*
1 teaspoon cornflour
1 teaspoon sugar
*3 tablespoons groundnut
    oil*
*4 spring onions, sliced
    diagonally*

1 clove garlic, crushed
*1 tablespoon chopped fresh
    root ginger*
*1/2 cucumber, sliced thinly,
    then shredded*
*175 g (6 oz) Chinese leaf,
    sliced thinly*
*175 g (6 oz) Cos or Webb's
    lettuce, sliced thinly*
*2 tablespoons chopped
    coriander leaves*
pepper to taste

Serves 4
Preparation time:
6 minutes
Cooking time:
4 minutes
Freezing:
Not recommended

1.   Blend together the soy sauce, sherry, stock or water, cornflour, sugar, and pepper. Set aside.
2. Heat the oil in a wok, add the spring onions, garlic, ginger and cucumber and stir-fry for 1 minute.
3. Add the Chinese leaf and lettuce and stir-fry for 1–2 minutes.
4. Pour in the blended sauce, stirring until thickened.
5. Transfer to a warmed serving dish, sprinkle with the coriander leaves and serve immediately.

THREE LEAF SALAD WITH HOT WALNUT SOY DRESSING

Another East meets West idea where the vegetables are served raw. A good side dish if you're serving several others, as the vegetables can be prepared well ahead.

*1/4 head Chinese leaf,
    shredded*
*350 g (12 oz) red cabbage,
    shredded*
1/2 bunch watercress
125 g (4 oz) bean sprouts
3 spring onions, chopped
*1 orange, peeled and cut
    into chunks*
FOR THE DRESSING:
*4 tablespoons groundnut
    oil*
2 tablespoons sesame oil

1 clove garlic, crushed
*2 tablespoons chopped
    fresh root ginger*
50 g (2 oz) walnut pieces
*3 tablespoons light soy
    sauce*
2 tablespoons dry sherry
*2 tablespoons wine
    vinegar*
2 teaspoons clear honey
*salt and Szechwan
    peppercorns, roasted
    and ground, to taste*

1. Mix the salad ingredients together in a large salad bowl. Season well with salt and Szechwan pepper.
2. Heat the oils in a small pan, add the garlic and ginger and stir-fry for 1 minute. Add the walnuts and stir-fry for 30 seconds, then stir in the remaining ingredients. Bring to the boil, pour over the salad, toss and serve immediately.

Serves 4–6
Preparation time:
10 minutes
Freezing:
Not recommended

DESSERTS

Although there are a number of Chinese sweet dishes, they tend to be eaten more as sweetmeats or treats. More often than not, a Chinese meal will end with fresh fruit—not served in an overflowing fruit bowl, but neatly prepared into pieces. The simplest idea is to choose a few fruits such as pears and oranges, slice into thin wedges and arrange alternately on a flat plate to resemble a star.

FRUITS ON A SNOW MOUNTAIN

Bite-size pieces of fruit nestling on crushed ice, to be served communally and picked at with chopsticks.

1 large ripe mango or paw-paw
1 small pineapple, peeled and cut into chunks
2 kiwi fruits, peeled and cut into chunks
2 pears, cored and cut into chunks
250 g (8 oz) lychees, peeled, or 425 g (15 oz) can, drained

400 g (14 oz) can loquats (medlars), drained (optional)
250 g (8 oz) strawberries
4 tablespoons medium dry sherry
about 1 kg (2 lb) crushed ice
fresh flowers to serve (optional)

Serves 6–8
Preparation time:
15 minutes
Freezing:
Not recommended

1. Cut the mango, if using, each side of the stone, then peel and cut into chunks. Quarter the paw-paw, if using, deseed, peel and cut into chunks.
2. Toss all the fruits in the sherry.
3. Mound two thirds of the ice on a large plate, then arrange the fruits around it, sprinkling the remaining ice in between.
4. Decorate the base with flowers, if you wish, to serve.

MELON BOWL WITH RED DATES

If you can't get dried red dates use ordinary fresh ones.

about 25 dried red dates
1 large Galia or other green-skinned melon
¼ water melon or small Charentais melon

1 piece preserved stem ginger, chopped
2 tablespoons preserved stem ginger syrup
1–2 tablespoons clear honey

1. If using dried dates, soak in hot water to cover for 3 hours; drain. Alternatively halve and stone fresh dates.
2. Cut off the top quarter of the Galia melon. Deseed all of the melon and scoop out as many balls as possible with a melon baller; reserve the juice. Scrape the inside of the shell.
3. Make melon balls with the water melon or Charentais. Mix both melons with the dates in a bowl.
4. Add the ginger, syrup, honey to taste, and reserved melon juice and toss well. Pile into the Galia melon shell and chill until required.

Serves 4–6
Preparation time: 15 minutes, plus soaking time
Freezing: Not recommended

INDEX

Photography by: Andy Seymour
Designed by: Sue Storey
Home economist: Lyn Rutherford
Stylist: Penny Legg
Illustration by: Linda Smith
Typeset by Rowland Phototypesetting Limited